SHREWSBURY TO NEWTOWN

Vic Mitchell and Keith Smith

MP Middleton Press

Front cover: No. 7336 waits to depart from Welshpool at 3.20pm on 31st March 1962, bound for Shrewsbury. In the bay platform is stock for a Whitchurch service. (H.Ballantyne)

Back cover: The east end of Shrewsbury station was recorded on 28th August 1989 as the 13.15 Cardiff to Liverpool runs in. The magnificent Abbey Church and historic signal box enhance the scene. (B.Robbins)

Published June 2008

ISBN 978 1 906008 29 1

© Middleton Press, 2008

Design Deborah Esher
Typesetting Barbara Mitchell

Published by
   Middleton Press
   Easebourne Lane
   Midhurst
   West Sussex
   GU29 9AZ
Tel: 01730 813169
Fax: 01730 812601
Email: info@middletonpress.co.uk
www.middletonpress.co.uk

Printed & bound by Biddles Ltd, Kings Lynn

INDEX

I. Railway Clearing House map for 1947.

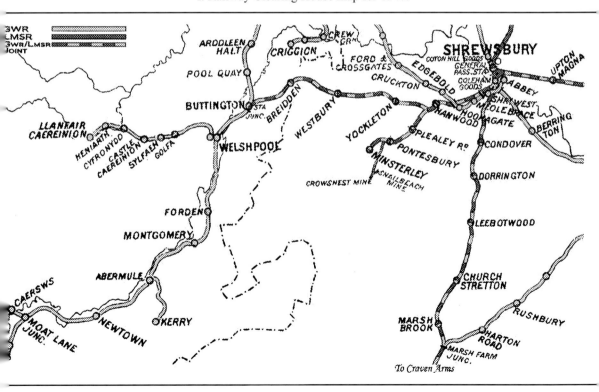

ACKNOWLEDGEMENTS

We are very grateful for the assistance received from many of those mentioned in the credits, also to P.G.Barnes, A.R.Carder, L.Crosier, G.Croughton, F.Hornby, S.C.Jenkins, D.K.Jones, N.Langridge, B.Lewis, A.Rhodes, Mr D. and Dr S.Salter, M.Turvey and in particular, our always supportive wives, Barbara Mitchell and Janet Smith.

GEOGRAPHICAL SETTING

We start close to the River Severn and also run near to it for the final 18 miles of our journey. The old part of the historic county town of Shrewsbury is bounded on three sides by the river and the station spans it.

The route climbs steadily over the northern flank of Long Mountain, the complex geology of which reaches a height of over 1000 ft. The summit of the line is west of Westbury station and soon the Shropshire/Montgomeryshire boundary is reached. (The latter became part of Powys in 1974.) This is also the boundary between England and Wales.

An undulating but steady, climb up the Severn Valley to Newtown follows, the underlying geology being sedimentary deposits of great age, described as Cambrian.

The maps are to the scale of 25ins to 1 mile, with north at the top, unless otherwise indicated.

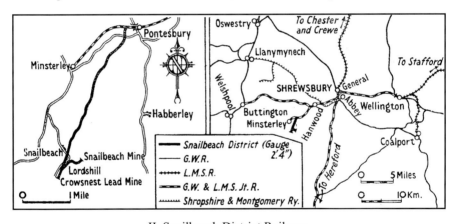

II. Snailbeach District Railway.

III. Gradient profile.

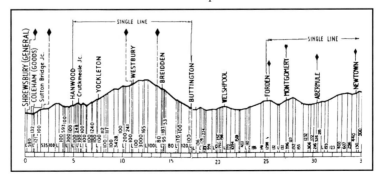

HISTORICAL BACKGROUND

Shrewsbury was served by the Shrewsbury & Chester Railway from 1848, the Shrewsbury & Birmingham Railway from 1849, the line north to Whitchurch from 1858 and the Shrewsbury & Hereford Railway opened south to Ludlow on 21st April 1852.

The Llanidloes & Newtown Railway was authorised in 1853 and opened in 1859. The Oswestry & Newtown Railway received its Act in 1855 and was opened south to Welshpool on 14th August 1860 and was completed to Newtown on 10th June 1861. The Newtown & Machynlleth Railway came into use in 1863 and all three railways were combined in 1864 to form the Cambrian Railways.

The Shrewsbury & Welshpool Railway was empowered to construct a route west to Buttington, this opening on 27th January 1862 and a line to Minsterley, which came into use first, on 14th February 1861. They were jointly operated by the Great Western and London & North Western Railways from 1865, as was the line to Hereford from 1870. The latter was known as the North and West Route. The Kerry branch was opened by the O&NR in July 1863.

The Cambrian was absorbed by the GWR in 1922 and the LNWR became part of the London Midland & Scottish Railway in 1923, but the GWR retained its identity. A joint operation of the North and West Route continued until nationalisation in 1948, as did the Shrewsbury - Buttington section. The same applied to the Minsterley branch.

All lines in the area became part of the Western Region of British Railways on 1st January 1948. The Minsterley branch closed to passengers on 5th February 1951 and to goods on 1st May 1967. The corresponding dates for the Kerry branch were 9th February 1931 and 1st May 1956. Our route was transferred to the London Midland Region on 17th June 1963.

Privatisation resulted in Central Trains operating services from 2nd March 1997. However, after reorganisation in October 2001, Wales & Borders became the franchisee. Arriva Trains Wales took over in December 2003.

Snailbeach District Railway

An Act of 5th August 1873 gave consent to build a line of 2ft 4ins gauge of about 5 miles in length to convey mainly lead ore to sidings on the Minsterley branch. The gradient was mostly 1 in 37, but a short branch was even steeper.

Lead mining ceased in about 1900, but carriage of stone and general goods continued for a while. Closure went unrecorded, but reopening took place in 1922 under the guidance of Lt. Col. H.F.Stephens, a light railway advocate of renown.

Most traffic subsequently was roadstone over a distance of about one mile (downhill) from Callow Hill Quarry to a coating plant and thus the extremities of the route were little used. Rail traffic ceased at the end of 1959 and a revival scheme began in 2008.

PASSENGER SERVICES

Throughout the CR era, timetables showed six weekday departures from Shrewsbury, with one or two more after 1910. Additionally, there were one or two more originating at Whitchurch or Oswestry. On Sundays, there were two until the early 1880s and one thereafter, over both routes.

The GWR takeover in 1922 brought few changes in the basic timetable, but the long-standing Tuesdays only market day train between Welshpool and Newtown continued only for a short while. The Sunday train made just two intermediate stops and ran from Oswestry.

The first BR timetable carried seven trains, all but two of which called at all stations and the Sunday one continued from the north. Little changed with transfer of the route from the WR to LMR in June 1963, but with the closure of the Whitchurch route in June 1965, the Sunday service was withdrawn and six weekday departures from Shrewsbury became the norm again.

A similar frequency has been maintained subsequently, but with Sunday trains being Summer only in most years.

Minsterley Branch

From the opening until about 1930, there were generally four return trips, weekdays only, all originating at Shrewsbury. Subsequently, the number rose to six, but it was finally four. There were extra Saturday trains in later years and even one on Sundays in the 1930s.

Kerry Branch

The initial timetable showed four return trips, with some extras in the Summer. It seems that Sunday trains were never operated. There were five trips in later years, but for most of the life of the line the figure was three, with extras on certain market days.

June 1869

February 1890

July 1910

November 1930

June 1950

February 1890

June 1869

ABERMULE and KERRY.—Cambrian.

Miles	Down.		Week Days.							Up.		Week Days.			
		mrn	noon	aft					Miles		mrn	aft	aft		
	Abermule..........dep	10 15	12 0	4 30						Kerry..........dep	9 0	11 0	3 50		
3¾	Kerry..........arr	10 40	12 25	4 55					3¾	Abermule 465, 467 arr	9 25	11 45	4 15		

ABERMULE and KERRY (3rd class only).

Miles	Down.	Wk Dys only				Miles	Up.	Wk Dys only				NOTES.
		mrn		aft	aft			mrn	mrn		aft	
	Abermule..........dep	1010		2 25	4 30		Kerry..........dep	8 55	1130		3 30	
1¼	Fronfraith..........	Hh		Hh	Hh	1¼	Goitre..........	Hh	Hh		Hh	Hh Stop when required.
2¼	Goitre..........	Hh		Hh	Hh	2¼	Fronfraith..........	Hh	Hh		Hh	
3¾	Kerry..........arr	1035		2 50	4 55	3¾	Abermule 136, 138..arr	9 20	1155		3 55	

WHITCHURCH, OSWESTRY, WELSHPOOL, SHREWSBURY, LLANIDLOES, MACHYNLLETH, ABERYSTWYTH, DOLGELLEY, BARMOUTH, PWLLHELI, &c.—Cambrian, & Shrewsbury & Welshpool Joint.

Gen. Man., George Lewis, Oswestry.] [Eng., Geo. Owen, Oswestry.

h Stop to set down from Stations on London and North Western, Mid Wales, and Great Western and beyond, on informing Guard at preceding *stopping Station.*

SHREWSBURY

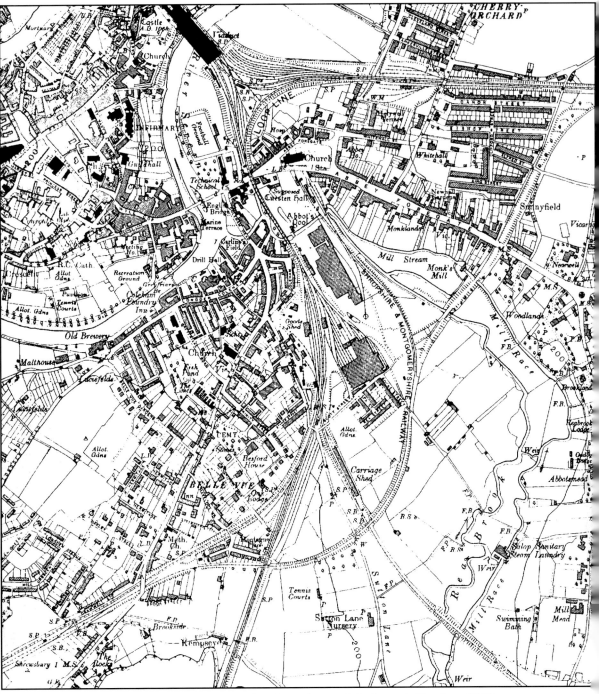

IV.   The 1929 survey at 6ins to 1 mile has the station top left, the main line from Wellington top right, the Severn Valley line lower right, the route to Ludlow and Hereford lower left. We will travel on the upper of the two lines on the left; the other is marked SHROPSHIRE & MONTGOMERYSHIRE RAILWAY and it terminates near the Abbey Church. The trackbed upper right linking this route with the Wellington line carried the line of the Potteries, Shrewsbury & North Wales Railway, which was in use in 1866-80. The S&MR is the subject of our *Branch Line to Shrewsbury* and maps therein feature the two engine sheds, and also Coleham Goods Yard, in 1882 and 1927.

1.   Known as "United Station" owing to its joint management by committee, it was unusual in its early years in having a superintendent, rather than a station master. The Tudor Gothic style building was extended on the left in 1854 and is seen undergoing major alterations around 1900, when the road was dug away and the entrance made into the former basement. A subway was created at this time. (A.Dudman coll.)

2.   Additional platforms were created in 1861-63 and extensive roofing followed. Part of it is seen in 1927, along with 4-4-0 no. 3277 *Earl of Devon* (later no. 3270). The northern part of the overall roof was removed in 1931-32. The station was known as "General" for much of the GWR era. (P.Q.Treloar coll.)

3.	Entering the south end on 29th June 1962 is 0-6-0 no. 3204 with the 7.35am from Aberystwyth. In the background is the massive signal box, which was opened by the LNWR in 1903 and named Severn Bridge. Please also see the back cover picture. (B.W.L.Brooksbank)

4.	Class 4300 2-6-0 no. 7330 waits in a bay platform (no. 5) on 3rd August 1962, ready to depart at 6.30pm. Arrival time at Aberystwyth would be 9.30 and it would stop at all stations except Dovey Junction. (E.Wilmshurst)

5.   Top left is the Abbey Church and the mighty signal box. Both were still busy in 2008. The River Severn passes across this undated picture and runs under the southern end of the platforms. The overall roof in this area was removed in 1963. Centre is the castle and to the left of it is the Dana footbridge, which passed over the entire station. (D.Richards/M.Dart coll.)

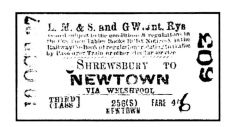

L. M. & S. and G.W. Jnt. Rys
Issued subject to the conditions & regulations in
the Cos. Time Tables Books Bills Notices & in the
Railway Clearing Book of regulations relating to traffic
by Passenger Train or other similar service
SHREWSBURY   TO
NEWTOWN
VIA WELSHPOOL
THIRD   256(S)   FARE 4/6
(CLASS)   NEWTOWN

6.   The replacement platform canopies are seen on 20th June 1966, as 4-6-0 no. 75048 waits to depart at 14.30 with the down "Cambrian Coast Express". From 1951, all such trains from London reversed here, instead of using the east side of the triangular junction. (H.C.Casserley)

7.   The view from the signal box on 14th September 1981 features no. 25141 approaching the platforms from the south with stone hoppers, which had been loaded at Bayston Hill Quarry. On the left is the east-south curve and the rear of the train is at English Bridge Junction. (B.Morrison)

8.   The 09.20 Euston departure was the "Cambrian Coast Express" on Summer Saturdays in 1989; the name was introduced in 1927. No. 37426 was recorded on the last day of operation, 30th September 1989. It ran in the Summer of 1990 as "The Snowdonian", but there were no such through trains thereafter. (D.A.Johnson)

9.   After the steam days ended, most trains for the Cambrian Coast terminated here. Standing at platform 6 on 12th September 1992 is a class 158 destined for Aberystwyth. Subsequently, there have been many through services from Birmingham, all reversing here. (T.Heavyside)

SOUTH OF SHREWSBURY

Engine Shed

10. The companies had separate sheds and the 1877 one of the GWR was to the east of the LNWR's of 1880. The former is seen on 21st July 1954 with ex-ROD 2-8-0 no. 3041 nearest. The building contained a turntable and was thus known operationally as "a roundhouse". From September 1963, the LMR took control of the sheds and the line southwards for 18 miles. (B.Morrison)

➜ 11. Seen on the same day outside the ex-LNWR shed is "Patriot" class 4-6-0 no. 45501 *St. Dunstans* on the 70ft turntable. Steam traction ceased here in March 1967, but the site was used for diesels for about another five years. There had been 120 locomotives allocated here in 1950. (B.Morrison)

Sutton Bridge Junction

➜ 12. Approaching the junction on 10th August 1985 are nos 37257 and 37235 with the 07.30 from Euston, "Cambrian Coast Express". This was the first Summer that this class had been employed on this task. On the right is the site of the engine sheds and in the background is the historic Abbey Church. (H.Ballantyne)

13.   Seen from the same bridge on 6th April 1974 is no. 5076 with the breakdown train. The sidings on the left served Coleham Goods Yard until its closure on 15th August 1966. The foot crossing in the foreground leads to the signal box. (T.Heavyside)

Other views of the station, the sheds and the junctions can be found in *Kidderminster to Shrewsbury* and *Shrewsbury to Ludlow*.

14.   We now have two views south of the bridge, showing the line to Newtown curving right. This is a stopping train from Welshpool hauled by ex-LNWR 0-6-2T no. 27640 on 21st June 1947. (H.C.Casserley)

15.   The 09.45 from Birmingham New Street has portions for Barmouth and Aberystwyth and is seen on 17th July 1976, running onto the single line. The double track Ludlow route and the goods loops are on the left. (T.Heavyside)

West of Sutton Bridge Junction

16.   This view east is from the left border of the Shrewsbury map (IV) and has the former down trackbed in the foreground. Nos 25162 and 25322 are heading the 09.35 Euston to Aberystwyth on 17th July 1976. Shrewsbury West platform was on the S&M from 1911 to 1933 and beyond the right border. (T.Heavyside)

MEOLE BRACE

17.   Featured is the track of the PS&NWR, that of the GWR & LNWR being on the left. The former had closed in 1880, long before this postcard was produced. Exchange sidings were provided here when the line reopened as the S&MR on 13th April 1911, as did a platform here on that line. Passenger service on the route ceased on 6th November 1933. (R.S.Carpenter coll.)

Va.   The 1927 edition shows the extent of the exchange sidings and the position of the gates. The S&MR lines are the lower ones. The signal box had 17 levers and was in use between 1911 and 1947.

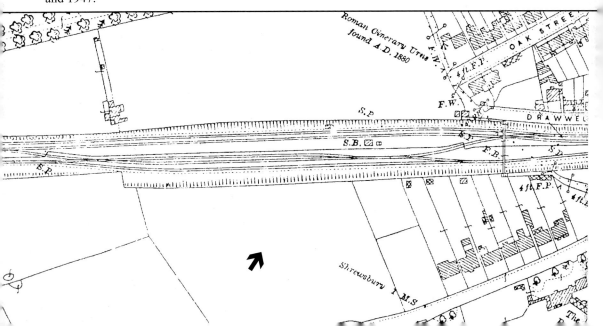

18.   Running alongside the former S&MR line is ex-Lancashire & Yorkshire Railway 2-4-2T no. 50781 piloting ex-GWR "Dukedog" 4-4-0 no. 9021 on a Talyllyn Railway Preservation Society special. It is seen from the footbridge on 29th September 1957. (Ted Hancock Books)

HOOKAGATE

← 19. Our route is on the other side of the fence in this 1937 westward view. The S&MR was requisitioned by the Army in 1941 to serve ammunition depots. This station was destroyed and spacious exchange sidings were laid out in this area. Their use declined in the 1950s, but they were used for a Long Rail Welding Depot from 1959 to 1986. (R.S.Carpenter coll.)

Other views of the S&MR route can be found in our *Branch Line to Shrewsbury* in pictures 99-110.

← 20. The depot was used to service ex-GWR no. 6000 *King George V* on 16th September 1972, after working the "Return to Steam" special between Newport and Shrewsbury. The locomotive was based at the Bulmers Centre at Hereford. (T.Heavyside)

21. Rails await welding on 14th July 1984, as nos 25279 and 25287 pass with the 10.10 Aberystwyth to Euston train, which they will work as far as Wolverhampton. Also evident is Hookagate signal box, which had 24 levers and was in use from about January 1942 until 18th November 1973. (H.Ballantyne)

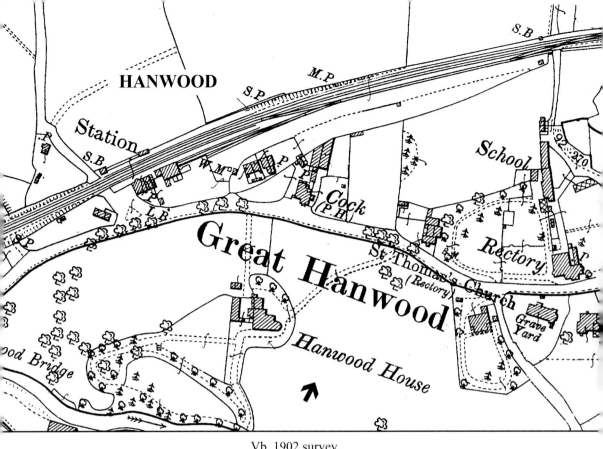

Vb. 1902 survey.

22.   The station opened earlier than the others on the route, as it was served by Minsterley trains. There was a small coalfield in the vicinity in the late 19th century. (Stations UK)

23.	A train from Aberystwyth calls in about 1957, headed by 0-6-0 no. 2286. The goods yard was in use until 6th May 1964, but passenger service was withdrawn on 12th September 1960. The population was only 515 by 1961. (J.W.T.House/C.L.Caddy)

24.	The signal box shows evidence of extension; this took place in 1954, when the frame size was increased from 16 to 35 levers. It was downgraded to a ground frame in 1963; the photograph is from 1958. The single line westward began here. (H.C.Casserley)

Minsterley Branch
CRUCKMEOLE JUNCTION

← 25. Short Hill Colliery was nearby and there were a number of other small pits in the area. The photograph is from about 1953 and features the Minsterley branch curving left. The box had 32 levers and opened in 1907. (P.J.Garland/R.S.Carpenter)

Table 184 WHITCHURCH, OSWESTRY, WELSHPOOL, and ABERYSTWYTH

Miles from Whitchurch		Week Days																			Suns.
		p.m	a.m	a.m	a.m	a.m	a.m	a.m	p.m	a.m	p.m	p.m	a.m	p.m	p.m	p.m	p.m	p.m			p.m
	London (Euston)..... dep	10 50	..	..	..	12 2	..	10 0	..	..	12 5	..	..	2 30	3‡45	3‡45	..	3 45	..	Sat. ngt.	9 25
	Manchester (L.R)..... "	12a30	..	..	..	5 45	7 15	12 15	..	..	1 18	3‡ 0	..	4 30	7‡10	7‡10	..	7 10	..		11 55
	Liverpool (L. St)..... "	12 5	..	..	..	..	..	11 40	..	..	1S5	2‡50	..	4 21	7‡5	7‡5	..	7 5	..		11 45
	Crewe..... "	2 15	..	..	..	7 32	8 37	1 22	..	..	3 18	4‡ 9	..	6 10	8‡15	8‡15	..	8 15	..		2 15
—	Whitchurch..... dep	3 15	..	..	..	8 17	9 55	2 5	..	..	4 5	..	..	6 50	..	..		9 20	..	Sunday morn.	3 15
3	Fenn's Bank.....	a.m	..	..	..	8 24	10 2	2 12	..	..	4 12	..	..	6 57	..	..	Saturdays only	9 27	..		..
6¼	Bettisfield.....	..	..	..	..	8 32	1010	2 19	..	..	4 23	..	..	7 5	..	..		9 35	..		..
7¾	Welshampton.....	..	..	..	..	8 36	1014	2 24	..	..	4 27	..	..	7 9	..	..		9 39	..		..
10¼	Ellesmere.....	3 36	..	..	..	8 44	1022	2 33	..	..	4 36	..	..	7 19	..	..		9 49	..		3 36
12¾	Frankton.....	..	..	..	..	8 49	1027	2 38	..	..	4 41	..	..	7 24	..	..		9 54	..		..
16¼	Whittington (High Level).....	..	..	..	..	8 57	1035	2 47	..	..	4 50	..	..	7 33	..	..		10 3	..		3 49
17¼	Tinker's Green Halt ¶.....	Aa	..	..	..	9 1	1038	2 51	..	..	4 53	..	..	7 37	..	..		10 7	..		..
18¼	Oswestry ¶..... arr	3 50	..	..	..	9 6	1042	2 55	..	..	4 57	..	..	7 41	..	..		1010	..		3 55
—	153 London (Pad.)..... dep	..	12a5	..	..	..	..	9R10	..	11R10	..	..	11R45	2 10	..	..	4 10	..	..		12 5
—	153 Manchester (Ex)..... "		..	..	..	..	..	11 45	..	..	1 35	..	..	5P 7	..	..	5 35	..	..		..
—	153 Birkenhead (W.)..... "	11H‡10	..		6 30	..	8 45	1 10	..	..	2 40	4‡33	4 33	5 35	7‡12	7‡12	7 12	..	..		11s‡10
—	153 Chester..... "	12H‡20	..		7 10	..	9 25	1 50	..	..	3 20	5‡10	5 10	6 25	7‡55	7‡55	7 55	..	..		12s‡20
—	Oswestry..... dep	4 5	7 50	..	8 20	..	1050	3 5	..	3 45	5 10	..	6 20	8 5			9 10	..	..	..	7 15
22	Llynclys.....	..	7 57	..	..	..	1057	3 12	..	3 52	5 17	..	6 27	8 12	Saturdays only	Except Saturdays	9 17	..	..	..	a.m
23¼	Pant (Salop).....	..	8 0	..	..	..	11 0	3 15	..	3 55	5 20	..	6 30	8 15			9 20	..	..	..	..
24¼	Llanymynech.....	4 16	8 4	..	8 30	..	11 5	3 20	..	3 58	5 24	..	6 33	8 20			9 23	..	..	..	7 25
32¾	190 Llanfyllin..... arr	..	..	..	8 57	..	1138	..		4 24	..	..	6 59	8E50			9 51	..	..	..	..
25¾	Four Crosses.....	..	8 8	..	8 34	..	11 9	3 24	Except Saturdays, or when Newtown School is closed	Stop	5 32	..	..	8 24			..	..	..	..	7 30
27¾	Arddleen.....	..	Stop	..	8 39	..	..	3 32			5 36	..	..	8 28			..	..	..	..	..
29¼	Pool Quay.....	..		..	8 44	..	1117	3 37		..	5 41	..	..	8 33			..	..	..	..	..
31¼	Buttington.....	..	..	..	8 50	..	1123	3 43		..	5 46	..	..	8 38			..	..	..	..	..
33¾	Welshpool..... arr	4 35	..	..	8 55	..	1128	3 48		a.m	5 52	..	..	8 44			..	..	..	..	7 45
—	153 London (Pad.)..... dep	..	..	..	12a5	..	..	11R10		11R10	..	2 10	..	..	4V10	5x10	..	..	..	..	12s5
—	" (Euston)..... "	9H25	p.m	..	..	..	..	..		..	..	..	..	..	5 5	5 5	..	..	..	..	..
—	153 Birmingham (S.H.)..... "	..		..	6 0	..	8 [illegible]2	1R43		1R43	..	4 45	..	..	7 0	7x41	..	..	..	..	4 10
—	" (N. St.)..... "	11H5		..	..	..	..	..		..	..	..	..	..	6 24	6 24	..	..	..	..	..
—	153 Wolverh'pton (L.L.) "	..	..	..	6 30	..	9 0	2R9		2R9	..	5 11	..	..	8 30	8 30	..	..	..	..	4 40
—	Mls Shrewsbury..... dep	3 48	..	..	7 55	..	1030	3 10		3 40	..	6 30	..	..	9 42	9 42	..	..	..	..	5 43
—	4¾ Hanwood.....	..	..	..	8 5	..	1040	..		3 50	..	6 40	..	..	9 55	9 55	..	..	..	..	Via Oswestry
—	7½ Yockleton.....	..	..	..	8 12	..	1045	..		3 56	..	6 47	..	..	10 2	10 2	..	..	..	..	
—	11 Westbury.....	..	..	..	8 22	..	1058	..		4 5	..	6 56	..	..	1011	1011	..	..	..	..	
—	13¼ Plas-y-Court Halt.....	..	..	..	8 28	..	11 4	..		4 10	..	7 2	..	..	1017	1017	..	..	..	..	
—	14 Breidden.....	..	..	..	8 32		11 8	..		4 15	..	7 7	..	..	1021	1021	..	..	..	..	
—	17 Buttington.....	..	..	..	8 33	..	1114	..		4 22	..	7 14	..	..	1027	1027	..	..	..	..	
—	19¾ Welshpool..... arr	4 25	..	..	8 43	..	1120	3 55		4 27	..	7 19	..	..	1032	1032	..	..	—	..	
—	Welshpool..... dep	4 45	..	..	9 0	..	1135	4 0	..	4 35	..	7 25	..	8 50	..	..	..	..	..	..	7 48
38½	Forden.....	..	..	..	9 8	..	1145	..	..	4 43	..	7 33	..	8 58	..	..	..	..	..	..	..
40	Montgomery.....	4 57	..	..	9 14	..	1150	4 12	..	4 48	..	7 39	..	9 3	..	..	..	..	..	..	8 0
43¾	Abermule.....	..	..	..	9 22	..	1158	..	..	4 58	..	7 47	..	9 11	..	..	..	..	..	..	8 8
47¾	Newtown.....	5 15	..	..	9 32	..	12 8	4 26	4 35	5 8	..	7 57	..	9 20	..	..	..	..	..	..	8 18
52¼	Moat Lane Junction..... arr	5 22	..	..	9 40	..	1216	4 34	4 43	5 16	..	8 5	..	9 29	..	..	..	..	..	..	..
59¾	185 Llanidloes..... arr	6 2	..	..	1011	..	1242	5 2	5 2	5 46	..	8 26	..	9 47	..	..	..	..	..	..	..
112¼	185 Brecon..... "	10 21	..	..	1238	..	5 24	..	..	8 11	..	..	..	..	..	..	..	..	..	..	..
—	Moat Lane Junction..... dep	5 27	..	..	9 50	..	1218	4 36	4 44	5 20	..	8 7	..	..	..	..	..	..	..	..	..
53½	Caersws.....	5 31	..	..	9 53	..	1222	..	4 47	5 23	..	8 10	..	..	..	..	..	..	..	..	8 32
55	Pontdolgoch.....	..	..	..	9 58	..	1227	..	4 52	5 28	..	8 15	..	..	..	..	..	..	..	..	..
59¼	Carno.....	5 45	..	..	10 9	..	1237	..	5 2	5 38	..	8 25	..	..	..	..	..	..	..	..	8 45
61½	Talerddig.....	..	..	..	1014	..	1243	..	5 8	5 44	..	8 31	..	..	..	..	..	..	..	..	..
64¾	Llanbrynmair.....	5 57	..	..	1020	..	1250	..	5 16	5 51	..	8 38	..	..	..	..	..	..	..	..	8 56
68¼	Commins Coch Halt.....	..	..	..	1028	..	1257	..	5 23	5 53	..	8 45	..	..	..	..	..	..	..	..	..
70	Cemmes Road.....	6 8	..	..	1033	..	1 2	..	5 28	6 4	..	8 50	..	..	..	..	..	..	..	..	9 6
75	Machynlleth..... arr	6 15	a.m	..	1041	..	1 10	5 12	5 36	6 12	..	8 58	..	..	..	..	..	..	..	..	9 15
	Machynlleth..... dep	6 22	8 10	..	1045	..	1 13	5 17	..	6 20	..	9 0	..	..	..	..	..	..	..	..	9 20
79	Dovey Junction..... arr	..	8 17	..	11 0	..	1 29	..	..	6 27	..	..	..	..	..	..	..	..	..	..	..
88½	189 Towyn..... arr	7*13	8 51	..	1138	..	2 0	6†9	..	7 32	..	..	..	..	..	..	..	..	..	..	10d1
100½	189 Barmouth..... "	7*47	9 24	..	1215	..	2 36	6†38	..	8 7	..	..	..	..	..	..	..	..	..	..	10d31
132¾	189 Pwllheli..... "	9* 9	1055	..	2 1	..	4 10	8†12	..	9 45	..	..	..	..	..	..	..	..	..	..	..
—	Dovey Junction..... dep	..	..	8 25	11 5	..	1 32	..	..	6 45	..	..	..	..	..	..	..	..	..	..	..
79¾	Glandyfi.....	6 33	..	8 28	11 8	..	1 35	5 27	..	6 48	..	9 10	..	..	..	..	..	..	..	..	9 30
85¼	Ynyslas.....	..	..	8 38	1118	..	1 45	..	..	6 58	..	9 20	..	..	..	..	..	..	..	..	..
87¼	Borth.....	6 46	..	8 43	1123	..	1 50	5 40	..	7 3	..	9 27	..	..	..	..	..	..	..	..	9 43
89¾	Llandre.....	6 54	..	8 50	1130	..	1 57	5 47	..	7 10	..	9 34	..	..	..	..	..	..	..	..	9 51
91¾	Bow Street.....	6 58	..	8 54	1135	..	2 1	..	..	7 15	..	9 38	..	..	..	..	..	..	..	..	9 55
95¾	Aberystwyth..... arr	7 7	..	9 4	1145	..	2 11	6 0	..	7 25	..	9 50	..	..	..	..	..	..	..	..	10 5

a a.m.
Aa Calls to set down on Mondays and Tuesdays
d Dep. Machynlleth 9 30 a.m.
E Except Saturdays
H Except Sunday nights
P Dep. 4 30 p.m. on Saturdays

R Restaurant Car Train
S Saturdays only
s Saturday nights
V Buffet Car to Wolverhampton
x Restaurant Car between Paddington and Wolverhampton

* Dep. Machynlleth 6 40 a.m.
† Dep. Machynlleth 5 30 p.m.
‡ Via Shrewsbury
¶ Additional trains are run between Tinker's Green Halt and Oswestry —see local announcements

September 1948

← Vc. The 1946 edition at 2 ins to 1 mile has Minsterley and Snailbeach near the bottom. The closed stations of the S&MR are shown with open circles.

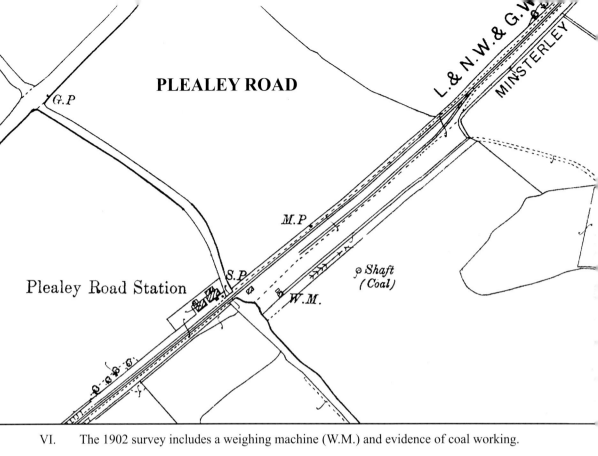

PLEALEY ROAD

L. & N.W. & G.W.

MINSTERLEY

G.P

M.P

Shaft
(Coal)

Pleasley Road Station

S.P

W.M.

VI.   The 1902 survey includes a weighing machine (W.M.) and evidence of coal working.

26.   We have five photographs from 22nd September 1958 and this includes the goods yard.
Passenger service on the branch had been withdrawn in 1951. A signal box was listed around 1900.
(H.C.Casserley)

PONTESBURY

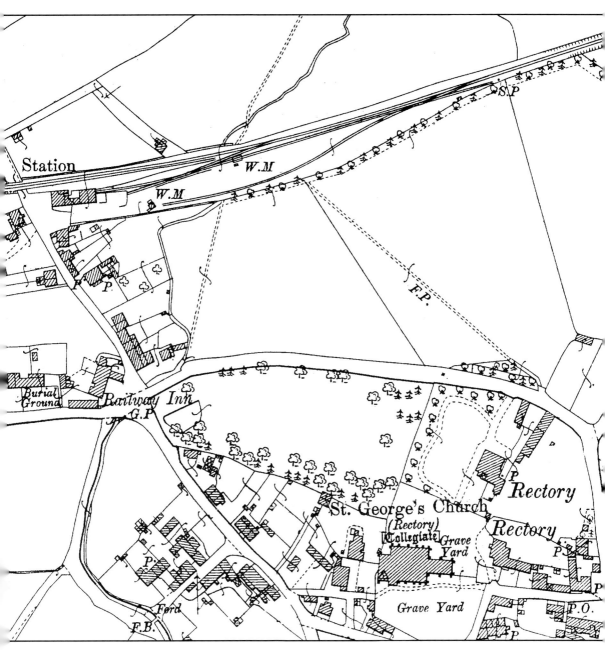

VII.   The 1902 edition reveals the proximity of the station to the centre of the village, which had a population of 2542 in 1901 and 3039 in 1961.

27.   This eastward view includes part of the goods yard and is from a departing goods train, again in 1958. (H.C.Casserley)

28.   A panorama in the other direction includes the goods shed, which contained a crane of the unusually low capacity of 15cwt. (H.C.Casserley)

WEST OF PONTESBURY

29.   A loop on the south side of the branch was provided for exchange traffic with the Snailbeach District Railway, but its track is concealed in the grass in this 1958 view. Its route is illustrated in pictures 40 to 48 herein. (H.C.Casserley)

30.   The branch curved southwest and passed over the lane to Asterley. The gates were worked by the train crew and there was a private siding for the Malehurst Barytes Company. It curves to the left. (R.M.Casserley)

MINSTERLEY

VIII. A 1902 survey reveals the closeness of the station to the centre of habitation, which was about 350ft above sea level.

Burial

F.B.

F.P.

Travelling Crane

Cranes

.C

Goods Shed

G W

.W

W.

W.

P

Oak House

P

.C

P

Station

The Poplars

P

Well

Minsterley

L.B.

Hotel G.P.

P.H.

Ind. Chap

P.H.

P

P

P

B.

P.

F.P.

S.P.

31.   The terminus and the steam saw mills were the subject of an early postcard view. There were 812 residents here in 1901. (Lens of Sutton coll.)

32.   A later postcard gave a balanced record of the structures and the loop. The signal box had 13 levers and was in use from about 1909 until 16th May 1954. (R.S.Carpenter coll.)

33.   The 2.0pm departure for Shrewsbury on 26th August 1946 was hauled by ex-LNWR 0-6-2T no. 7740. Alongside is 0-6-0 no. 28204, also ex-LNWR. (SLS coll.)

34.   A special train was organised on 23rd April 1955, the headboard showing "SLS The Shropshire Rail Tour MLS". The loco is 0-6-0 no. 2516, which was ex-GWR. (T.J.Edgington)

35.   The same train is seen again as photography continues. Note that the platform loop had gone by that time. The yard had a crane rated at 4½ tons capacity. (H.F.Wheeller/R.S.Carpenter)

36.   The entrance to the goods yard is evident in this panorama from 22nd September 1958, by which time the platform was also used for goods. (R.M.Casserley)

37.   The exterior was recorded on the same day, with a Ford 8 and Hillman 10 in attendance, both designs being from the 1930s. The population was under 900 when the line closed to passengers. (R.M.Casserley)

38. The final special ran on 12th September 1959 and it was the only occasion on which a DMU traversed the branch. The headboard was styled for boilers, not cats whiskers. (G.Adams/M.J.Stretton coll.)

39. The canopy was removed during the winter of 1958-59. An additional store building was erected and is seen in August 1961, as nature took over. (R.G.Nelson/T.Walsh)

SNAILBEACH DISTRICT RAILWAY

40.   We start our visit at the sidings near Pontesbury, where stone was discharged into the plant in which it was coated with tar for road making or repair. It was operated by Shropshire County Council. (H.F.G.Dalston)

41.   Near the sidings on 11th June 1943 is Kerr Stuart 0-4-2T no. 2 of 1902 with some of the 37 hopper wagons on the line. Two of the three flat wagons are evident as well. There were also 16 open wagons, two of which were bogies. (L.W.Perkins/F.A.Wycherley)

42.   The railway passed over the Shrewsbury-Bishops Castle A488 road on this slender bridge. It is seen in 1958, in the company of a Hillman Minx of 1934 vintage. In its final years, the line carried about 400 tons of stone each week. (H.C.Casserley)

43.   This is a view towards Pontesbury, near Minsterley, on 15th May 1929. The gauge on official returns was 2ft 3¾ins, but fortunately, sleeper length did not have to be specified. (R.M.Casserley coll.)

44.   Map II shows this connection near the terminus. Owing to the terrain it was necessary for trains to reverse to reach Snailbeach Perkins Level Mine and then to climb steeply. There had once been a siding for a smelter off this line. The photograph is from September 1941.
(R.S.Carpenter coll.)

45.   The engine shed was near the end of the line at Lordshill and three engines were maintained in working order in 1943, being used in rotation of about one month. Nearest is no. 2, already seen in picture 41. A Fordson tractor hauled the empty wagons from July 1946.
(L.W.Perkins/F.A.Wycherley)

46.   Behind is no. 4, a Baldwin 4-6-0T built in 1915 for use in World War I. The shelf at the back was for a hose for lifting water from streams and ditches. Two such engines were purchased in 1923. (L.W.Perkins/F.A.Wycherley)

47.   The other Baldwin was recorded on 15th September 1948. Both had been regauged from 1ft 11½ ins by Bagnall in 1918. A wooden extension had been provided to house the two extra engines, but the roof had long gone. (J.H.Moss/R.S.Carpenter coll.)

48.   Loaded wagons were often run down the line under gravity and so an engine was usually steamed on alternate days to recover them. The operational mile was two miles from the engine shed, which is seen in 1958. (R.M.Casserley)

YOCKLETON

IX.   The 1902 survey includes a pair of staff cottages at the east end of the small goods yard, which closed on 12th September 1960, the same day as passenger service was withdrawn.

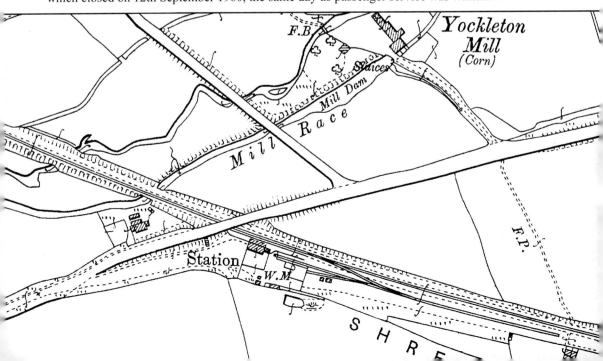

49.	Few could appreciate the splendid barge boards, unless walking along the road from Nox, the next small community east. Stone quoins and square chimney pots add to the charm. (Lens of Sutton coll.)

50.	A 1958 record features the east elevation and the bridge carrying the B4386. Staffing ceased on 2nd July 1956. (R.M.Casserley)

WESTBURY

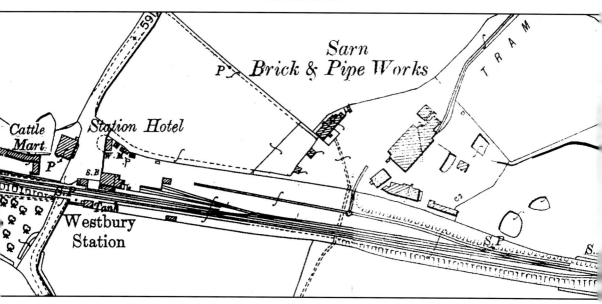

X. This 1902 extract includes the full length of the passing loop and a short siding into the adjacent works, which had its own rail system.

51. Many details are common with Yockleton, including the closure date to passengers. However, goods services continued until 15th March 1965. (Lens of Sutton coll.)

52.   The 10.35am Welshpool to Shrewsbury runs in on 23rd August 1948 behind 2-6-0 no. 6307. The tablet catchers are each side of it. For many years, tablets were used eastwards and a staff westwards. (H.C.Casserley)

53.   Included in this view from a down train are the level crossing and the cattle pens. This and the next picture are from the early 1950s. (R.S.Carpenter)

54.   The structure on the left carried the water tank. The locomotive is 4-6-0 no. 7828 *Odney Manor*, which was later preserved to reside on the West Somerset Railway. It is passing the ground signal for access to the goods yard via a trailing connection from the down loop. (SLS coll.)

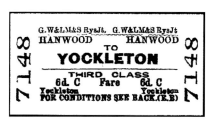

55.   No. 37426 enters the loop on 12th July 1986, with the 11.10 Aberystwyth to Euston, while no. 37430 waits with the 09.35 from Euston. Such an event could only be witnessed on Summer Saturdays. (B.Robbins)

56.   The box was built in about 1874 and the GWR fitted it with a 21-lever frame in 1915. Closure came on 21st October 1988, by which time passing had ceased and automatic half-barriers were in use. The photograph date is 12th July 1987. (C.L.Caddy)

PLAS-Y-COURT HALT

57.   The halt opened on 3rd November 1934 and closed on the same day as its neighbours. It is seen in August 1961. Trains pass into Wales west of this location. (R.G.Nelson/T.Walsh)

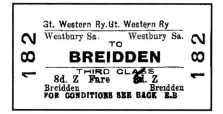

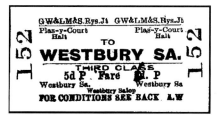

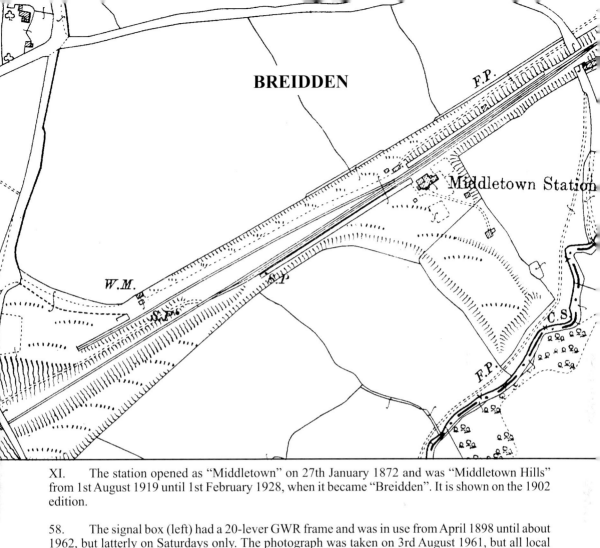

BREIDDEN

Middletown Station

W.M.

F.P.

F.P.

F.P.

C.S.

XI. The station opened as "Middletown" on 27th January 1872 and was "Middletown Hills" from 1st August 1919 until 1st February 1928, when it became "Breidden". It is shown on the 1902 edition.

58. The signal box (left) had a 20-lever GWR frame and was in use from April 1898 until about 1962, but latterly on Saturdays only. The photograph was taken on 3rd August 1961, but all local traffic had ceased on 12th September 1960. (R.G.Nelson/T.Walsh)

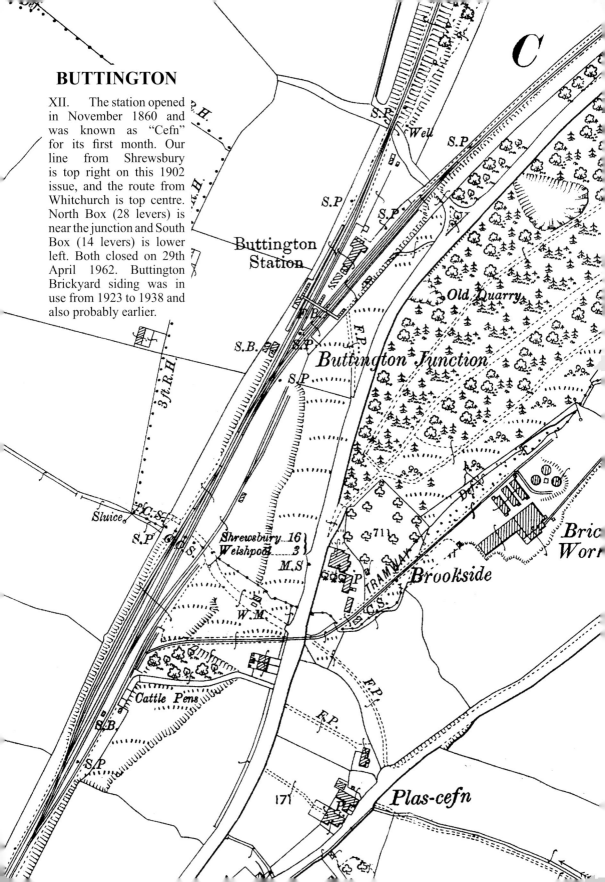

BUTTINGTON

XII. The station opened in November 1860 and was known as "Cefn" for its first month. Our line from Shrewsbury is top right on this 1902 issue, and the route from Whitchurch is top centre. North Box (28 levers) is near the junction and South Box (14 levers) is lower left. Both closed on 29th April 1962. Buttington Brickyard siding was in use from 1923 to 1938 and also probably earlier.

C

Well

S.P.

S.P.

S.P.

S.P.

Buttington Station

S.P.

Old Quarry

F.P.

S.B.   S.P.

Buttington Junction

S.P.

3 ft. R.H.

F.P.

Def.

Sluice

P.C.S.

S.P.   G.S.

Bric
Worr

71

Shrewsbury 16
Welshpool 3

M.S.

S.P.   TRAMWAY   *Brookside*

C.S.

W.M.

Cattle Pens

S.B.

F.P.

F.P.

S.P.

171

Plas-cefn

59.   A train bound for Shrewsbury runs into the joint line platform; the junction with the Cambrian Railways is in the background. Note the evidence of platform lengthening. (Lens of Sutton coll.)

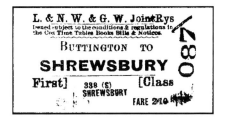

60.　An eastward panorama from 9th August 1948 features former GWR 0-6-0 no. 3217 with the 6.30pm Shrewsbury to Aberystwyth. The loco was still fairly new at that time. (W.A.Camwell/SLS coll.)

61.　Looking south in 1954, we gain a glimpse of the sidings. There had been two parallel single tracks to Welshpool until 1893. (J.Hollick/A.Vaughan coll.)

62.   The footbridge was demolished in about 1957, by which time few passengers were changing trains here. Unlike the others, the platform for Oswestry trains is of timber construction. This was because it was built on marshland, as was much of the line to Welshpool. Settlement caused trains to creep along in the 1970s, when repair funds were short. (R.G.Nelson/T.Walsh)

EAST OF WELSHPOOL

63.   The line passes over the A458 about one mile from the junction at Buttington Crossing. The 16.43 from Shrewsbury is passing on 4th May 1983. The box had a 22-lever frame and opened on 24th September 1962. It controlled just the crossing from 8th October 1967; automatic half barriers came later. (P.Johnson)

XIII.   The 1953 edition at 6 ins to 1 mile has our route diagonally on the right. The 2ft 6ins gauge 1903 Welshpool & Llanfair Railway runs across the map, albeit indistinctly in the urban area. It closed to passengers in 1931 and to goods in 1963. It reopened in its preservation era to Raven Square (left) in 1982, but will never reach the main line station again.

64.   Leaving for the coast is 4-4-0 no. 3262, a "Duke" class in use in 1896-1937. The line had been doubled southward to Forden in July 1925. (P.Q.Treloar coll.)

65.   Standing with an up train is 4-4-0 no. 9028, the last of the 9000 class 4-4-0s to be built. A Rochester pattern gas lamp is included. (W.A.Camwell/SLS coll.)

XIIIa. Welshpool residents had the convenience of these trains at one time, but sadly the leaflet was not dated.

CAMBRIAN RAILWAYS.

THROUGH LAVATORY CARRIAGES

BY

Special Service of Express Trains,

RUN AS UNDER:

LONDON (Euston)	LIVERPOOL (Lime Street)
To Aberystwyth via Welshpool 9 §30, 11 0 a.m. and 2 35 p.m.	To Aberystwyth via Whitchurch, 8 15, 10 30, a.m., 12 10 and 3 25 p.m.
To Barmouth via Welshpool, 9 30 and 11 0 a.m.	From Aberystwyth via Whitchurch, 8 45 a.m., 12 5 noon, and 2 15 p.m.
To Criccieth via Welshpool, 9 30 and 11 0 a.m.	

69.   Taking water on 31st March 1962 is no. 7823 *Hook Norton Manor*. It is carrying the "Cambrian Coast Express" headboard. On the right is the yard's six-ton crane. (H.Ballantyne)

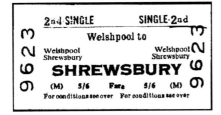

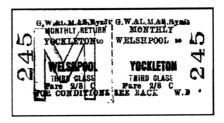

70.	A train from Shrewsbury is approaching on 19th January 1969 and is nearing the former North Box, which was built in 1897 and had a new 63-lever frame fitted in 1931 when South Box closed. Radio control of 130 miles of former CR lines was operative from 21st October 1988. (A.M.Davies)

71.	The splendid west facade was recorded on 18th May 1963, along with a classic Crossville bus. (P.Kingston)

72.   DMUs were introduced on the route in the early 1960s and units of this type were common for over 20 years. This is working the 15.45 Aberystwyth to Shrewsbury on 14th July 1965. Class 116 units were introduced in 1957. (C.L.Caddy)

73.   The last day of steam working of the route was recorded on 4th March 1967. There had been private sidings for Midland Tar Distillers, Boys & Boden and Smithfield Market. (A.M.Davies)

74.   There was an unusual event on 24th August 1986, when nos 25201 and 25037 called with the "Snowdonian II" railtour from Paddington to Pwllheli. The footbridge is unclear, as it had lost its roof by that time. (D.H.Mitchell)

75.   The 13.04 Aberystwyth to Birmingham on 7th September 1989 was formed of units 150116, 150142 and 150133, but unusually the leading one had only one coach. These platforms were removed and fresh ones were opened on 18th May 1992. The building later became a craft centre. (T.Heavyside)

76.   In order to create a bypass road, the tracks were moved away from the building and a new platform was constructed, together with a refuge siding. No. 158042 is working a Birmingham to Aberystwyth service on 13th June 2003. (P.Jones)

77.   This view in the same direction in 2007 is from the new footbridge. It is included to show the extent of its ramps and thus the length of the hike to the island platform. This is in the right background and the road is on the site of the main lines. (M.J.Stretton)

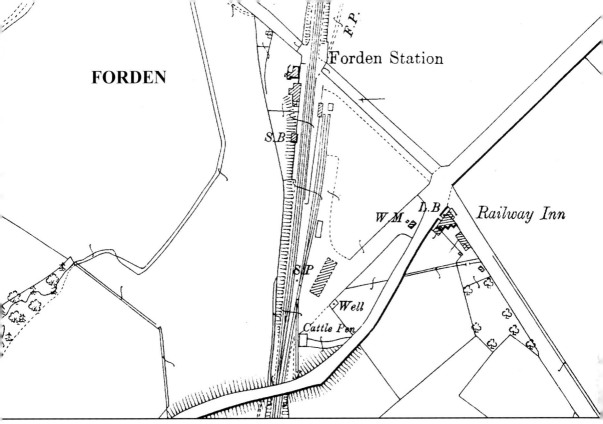

FORDEN

Forden Station

XIV.   The 1902 edition indicates the extent of the small goods yard, which was in use until 4th May 1964. The level crossing is at the top.

78.   A postcard panorama includes the 1897 signal box and the 1861 squat original building. The loop ends in the distance. The station served Brynhyfryd Hospital, ¼ mile to the south. (Lens of Sutton coll.)

79.   This southward view is from the level crossing on 27th July 1961. The local population grew from 681 in 1901 to 791 in 1961. Staffed only part time from 1957, it closed on 14th June 1965. (R.G.Nelson/T.Walsh)

80.   We look in the opposite direction on the same day and study the single line tablet equipment. There had been a serious accident here on 26th November 1904, when two trains collided head-on in the down platform due to driver error. (R.G.Nelson/T.Walsh)

81.   The box had a 22-lever frame and was unusual in not being close to the level crossing. It was photographed in July 1966, shortly before closure. (C.L.Caddy)

82.   The station house and the signal box were in private ownership when recorded in June 1993. The crossing had automatic half-barriers by that time. (B.W.L.Brooksbank)

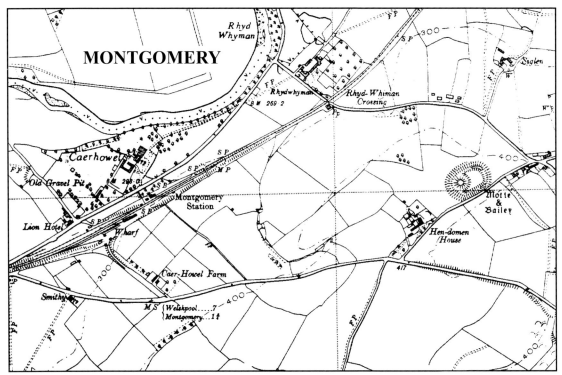

MONTGOMERY

XV. The 1953 map at 6 ins to 1 mile reveals the remote location of the station. It was almost two miles from the county town, which it served. This had only 1034 inhabitants in 1901; the figure dropped to 970 in 1961 and the county vanished in 1974.

83. The lengthy loop is evident on 27th July 1961, as is the point of extension of the original signal box in 1932, when the frame was enlarged from 15 to 30 levers. The box closed on 20th July 1969. (R.G.Nelson/T.Walsh)

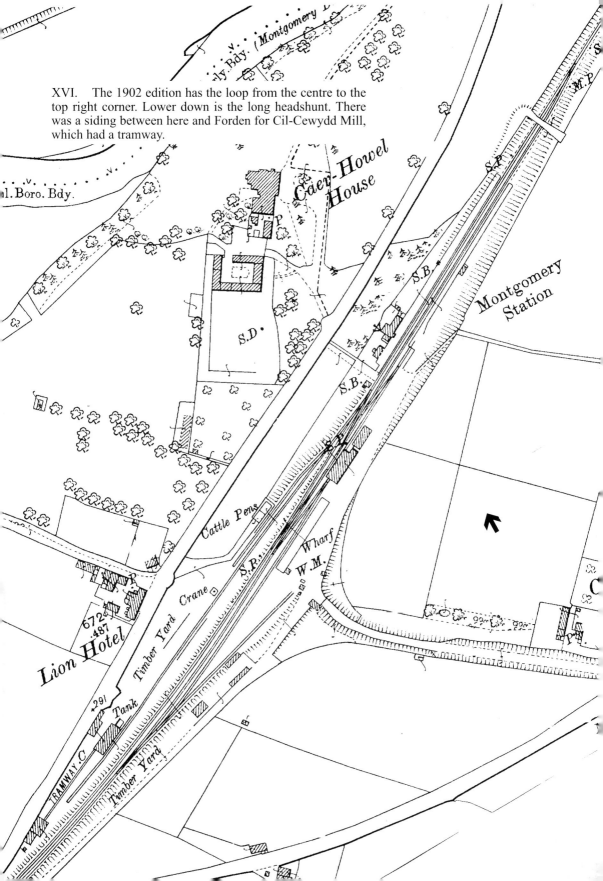

XVI.   The 1902 edition has the loop from the centre to the top right corner. Lower down is the long headshunt. There was a siding between here and Forden for Cil-Cewydd Mill, which had a tramway.

84.   Two "Manors" pass in an unusual manner in June 1962. The nearest records a SPAD, a modern term for a signal passed at danger, of no consequence in those days where no track circuits were present. The goods shed lasted into the 21st century. (A.M.Davies)

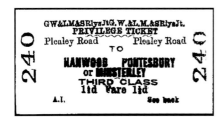

GW&LM&SRlysJtG.W.&L.M.&SRlysJt.
PRIVILEGE TICKET
Plealey Road   Plealey Road
TO
HANWOOD PONTESBURY
or MINSTERLEY
THIRD CLASS
1½d   Fare 1½d
A.I.   See back
240   240

2nd · SINGLE   SINGLE · 2nd
Montgomery to
Montgomery   Montgomery
Forden   Forden
FORDEN
(W)   5d.   Fare 5d.   (W)
For conditions see over For conditions see over
2102   2102

85.   Minutes later and the signal is "off" for the departure of the 9.45 Whitchurch to Aberystwyth. On the right is the disused dock, which had an end-loading facility. Goods traffic ceased here on 4th May 1964. (A.M.Davies)

86.   No. 46525 stands at the up platform on 30th May 1964, with the lengthy 8.20am Oswestry to Aberystwyth. The main building was erected in 1873. (E.Wilmshurst)

87.   The station had entrances on both sides of the track, but no footbridge was provided, passengers using the crossing in the foreground. The 10.10 Paddington to Pwllheli stands at the down platform on 20th August 1966. Although no. 75047 is devoid of the CCE headboard, it has whitened features and a red backed number plate. (D.A.Johnson)

88.   Passenger service was withdrawn on 14th June 1965 and the box, plus lamp room, were photographed in July 1966. The milepost reads 40¼, which was a Cambrian Railways measurement from Whitchurch. (C.L.Caddy)

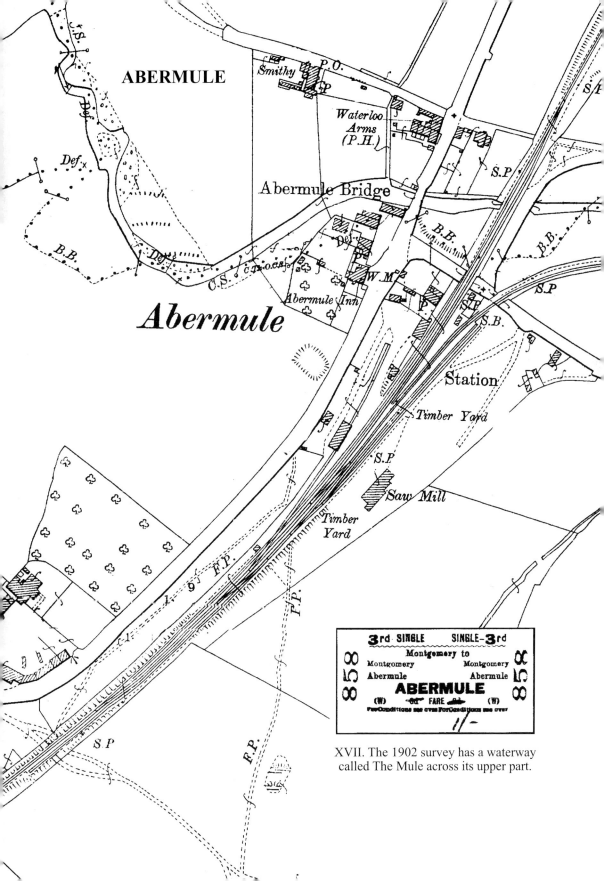

ABERMULE

Smithy

P.O.

Waterloo
Arms
(P.H.)

Abermule Bridge

Def

W.M.

Abermule Inn

Abermule

Def

B.B.

C.S.

Def

B.B.

B.B.

S.P.

S.P.

S.P.

S.B.

S.B.

Station

Timber Yard

S.P.

S.P.

Saw Mill

Timber
Yard

F.P.

F.P.

F.P.

S.P.

F.P.

3rd SINGLE   SINGLE-3rd
Montgomery to
Montgomery   Montgomery
Abermule   Abermule
ABERMULE
(W)   -6d- FARE   (W)
For Conditions see over For Conditions see over
1/-

858   858

XVII. The 1902 survey has a waterway
called The Mule across its upper part.

89.   Shunting the Kerry branch train at the north end of the station in about 1920 is Cambrian Railways 0-6-0T no. 26. The population of Kerry and district seldom justified more than one coach. Such traffic ceased in 1931. (R.S.Carpenter coll.)

90.   The branch platform was on a small radius curve, but this was of little consequence with the shortness of the passenger trains. No. 2343 is returning from Kerry with just a brake van, in about 1949. (W.A.Camwell/SLS coll.)

91.   We are at the same location, but looking in the other direction as another "Dean Goods" is about to depart for Kerry, sometime in the early 1950s. Its shed plate shows 89A, which indicates Oswestry as its base. (M.Whitehouse coll.)

92.   Departing for Shrewsbury in around 1952 is no. 9000, an ex-GWR 4-4-0 of the "Dukedog" class. This type was introduced in 1936 and carried the names of Earls; they were thus the "Earl" class initially and were numbered in the 3200 series. (W.A.Camwell/SLS coll.)

93.   No. 7802 *Bradley Manor* races towards the coast, while 0-6-0 no. 2556 waits on the Kerry line. The branch signal can be seen in this view, which is also from the early 1950s. The former avoided the scrap man and is resident on the Severn Valley Railway. (W.A.Camwell/SLS coll.)

94.   Both sets of level crossing gates are included in this panorama from the same era. The unusual level of sidings can be seen on the right. (Ted Hancock Books)

95.   The 9.45am Whitchurch to Aberystwyth stands in perfect lighting in June 1962, while hauled by no. 7827 *Lydham Manor*. The locomotive was preserved and arrived on the Dart Valley Railway in January 1970. (A.M.Davies)

96.   The connection to the branch and goods yard are clear; the former closed on 1st May 1956 and the latter on 4th May 1964. An up express speeds down the gradient behind no. 7803 *Barcote Manor*, sometime in 1963. (A.M.Davies)

97.   Bearing the CCE headboard, no. 7810 *Draycott Manor* disturbs the peace of this quiet junction as it roars up the valley, not long before the end of steam.
(A.J.B.Dodd/P.Chancellor coll.)

98.   No. 7821 *Ditcheat Manor* waits with the 7.35am Aberystwyth to Shrewsbury on 30th May 1964. The north end lean-to does not appear in the other photographs. (E.Wilmshurst)

99.   Passenger trains ceased to call on 14th June 1965, but the signal box remained in use until 9th October 1966, when it served as a ground frame. It was built in 1891 and had 14 levers. (C.L.Caddy)

Kerry Branch

XVIII. The 1952 edition includes the northern part of the branch, which is in woodland in a deep valley. The scale is 6 ins to 1 mile; the branch was 3¾ miles in length.

FFRONFRAITH HALT

100.   A 1931 northward view includes the siding for the mill, which is shown near the bottom of the map. (R.K.Cope/R.S.Carpenter)

101.   A closer look at D.C.Evans' mill in 1955 shows the 27ft long platform, which was reputedly never to carry a nameboard in CR days. The mill's doors have seen better days. (T.J.Edgington)

102.   The platform seems a little longer than the neighbouring one. Obscured in the grass in the distance is a brickworks siding. At 2¾ miles from Abermule, it was at the top of a long gradient up at 1 in 43. (T.J.Edgington)

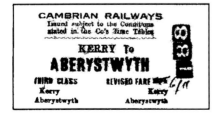

KERRY

103.   Posed at the terminus is CR no. 36 *Plasfynnon*, which was built by Sharp Stewart in 1863 for the Oswestry & Newtown Joint Committee. The coach appears to carry the words "Kerry Branch" between the door handles. Nos 37 and 38 also worked on the branch, but all three were withdrawn by 1907. (P.Q.Treloar coll.)

104.   The north elevation was fitted with fine barge boards and shapely finials. One paraffin lamp sufficed to illuminate the platform, which supports a stack of pullet crates. (SLS coll.)

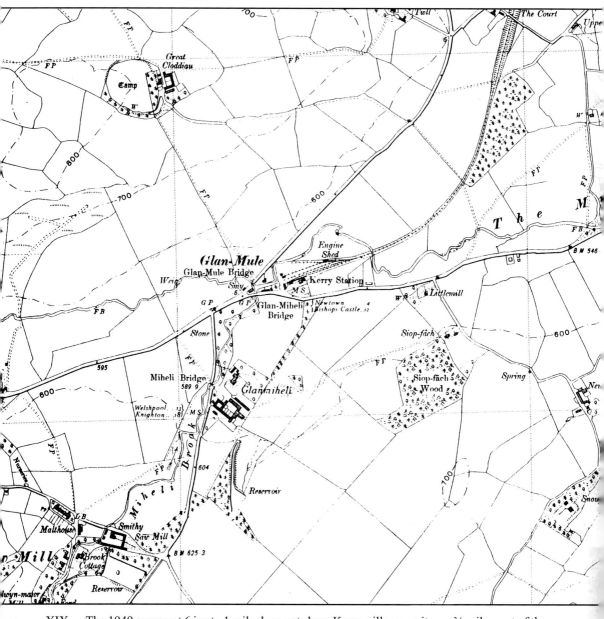

XIX.   The 1949 survey at 6 ins to 1 mile does not show Kerry village, as it was ¾ mile west of the station. The parish housed 1724 souls in 1901. There is no evidence of the five mile long forestry railway of 1ft 11½ ins gauge, which operated in 1888-95.

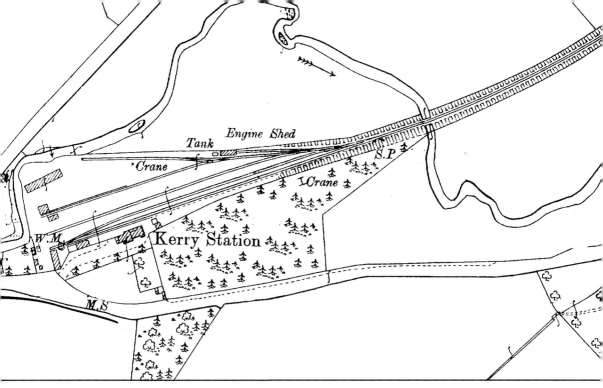

XX.   The 25ins scale 1902 survey indicates a turntable at the end of the platform line. In fact it was a sector plate and can be seen under the brake van in picture 103. The crane was recorded in 1938 as of six-ton capacity.

105.   We now have four photographs from around 1950. The finials have gone, but the exotic chimney pots remain to be enjoyed in a lull in the shunting. The "Toad" brake van is endorsed ABERMULE. (W.A.Camwell/SLS coll.)

106.   Apart from the loss of its ventilator, the engine shed seems intact structurally, although last used in 1931, when passenger service ceased. There was a freight train thrice weekly in the final years. Double heading was permitted and a single wooden staff provided safety. (P.J.Garland/R.S.Carpenter)

107.   A young railway observer notes that the "Dean Goods" is making up a train composed of mostly cattle wagons. In the background is the weighbridge office. (M.Whitehouse coll.)

108.   Items not seen so far are (from left to right) the loading gauge, the permanent way hut, the goods shed and the cattle dock. Track is less obvious. In the period 1931-39 there had been one passenger train a year; this was for Kerry Sunday School. (M.Whitehouse coll.)

109.   Working the branch on 4th April 1956 is the last functional "Dean Goods", no. 2538. All traffic would cease on 1st May following and the long trains for the Kerry Sheep Fair would be just a memory. (G.F.Bannister/M.Dart coll.)

WEST OF ABERMULE

110.   We return to the main line to look at the consequences of the Abermule disaster on 26th January 1921. The photographs were taken four days after the head-on collision between an express from Aberystwyth and a westbound stopping train. The crew of the latter had the wrong tablet after a muddle at the station; they died. Parts are sheeted as clearance continued with the help of 0-6-0 no. 31. (K.Nunn/LCGB)

111.   Telescoping of coaches led to the death of others, including the CR chairman. The other loco crew survived, having observed the oncoming train and escaped. There were 17 fatalities. Eastbound was 4-4-0 no. 95 and running to the coast was 4-4-0 no. 82. (K.Nunn/LCGB)

112.   The scale of the devastation was beyond words. The facts are that on the right is LNWR third class corridor coach no. 260, centre is the boiler of no. 82 and above it are the wheels and chassis of no 95. (A.Dudman coll.)

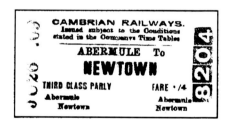

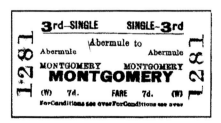

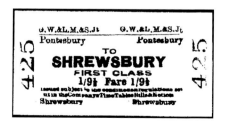

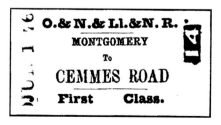

XXI.   The 1952 survey at 6ins to 1 mile shows two goods yards. The one lower left is on the site of the first station, which was opened by the Llanidloes & Newtown Railway in 1859. Newtown's gas company (centre) started as early as 1841 with coal brought by the 1821 Montgomeryshire Canal. 1729 tons were being carted from the railway by 1913, rising to about 2270 in 1950. Newtown, Rhayader, Builth Wells and Llanidloes were all reached by the Mid-Wales Gas Grid in 1959-60, removing 5000 tons of coal traffic from the railway. A similar tonnage of domestic coal was being consumed in these towns, but cheaper gas soon displaced almost all this trade, leaving little local mineral traffic for the railway.

113.   This is the town's third station building and dates from 1869. No. 2255 stands at the down through platform in about 1950. The 0-6-0 was built in 1930. (W.A.Camwell/SLS coll.)

114.   This 1954 record is a reminder of the days when Royal Mail used Morris Commercial vans to convey mailbags direct to and from the trains. (Stations UK)

115.   With frost on the crossing, no. 7803 *Barcote Manor* generates a steam background in the chill of a winter morning in 1963. The steam heating of its up train is also evident. (A.M.Davies)

Table 26

LONDON AND CAMBRIAN COAST

WEEK DAYS / SUNDAYS

	C	Z	RD A S	RD A S	R	R	R A	R A	R A	R A	A	CP	Z	A	C
	am	am	am	am	am	am	am	pm	pm	pm	pm	night	night	am / pm	night
PADDINGTON dep	12 5	1 0	10 10	10 50	11 0	11 10	11 55	2 10	4 10	5 10	9 25	12 5	10 0	12 5 / 9 25	12 5
Welshpool arr	8 43	...	2 0	2 56	3 50	4 32	...	7 19	10 32	10 32	...	8 43	...	7J15 / ...	8*43
Aberdovey	11 25	N	4 10	4 56	5 58	7 24	N	.	.	..	..	N	11 25	9K23 / N	11*25
Towyn	11 35	...	4 17	5 3	6 9	7 32	...	.	.	..	..	...	11 35	9K31 / ...	11*35
Aberystwyth	11 47	1‡16	4 5	5 10	5 50	7 25	7a54	9 46	..	..	8*30	11 47	1‡16	9J29 / 8*30	11*47

WEEK DAYS / SUNDAYS

	R	R	RD S	R	RD E	S	R	R	R G	R	B	M
	am	am	am	am	am	am	pm	pm	pm	pm	pm	pm
Aberystwyth dep	7 30	7 20	9A25	9 55	11A15	11c 0	12 5	12 45	1 48	2 30	5d35	6 0
Towyn	7 28	...	9A22	10 5	11A33	11 34	...	12 54	..	2 34	...	6 10
Aberdovey	7 35	N	9A31	10 11	11A40	11 44	N	..	N	2 45	N	6 17
Welshpool	10 0	...	11 55	12 30	1 55	1 48	...	3 10	..	5 20	...	8 50
PADDINGTON arr	2F12	3b10	4 10	5 15	6 0	6 20	7Y45	8 35	10 0	10 25	4*25	5V10

WEEK DAYS / SUNDAYS

	C	R T	R S	R E	RD E	RD S	R E	R S	R	CP	C
	am	am	am	am	am	am	am	am	pm	night	am
PADDINGTON dep	12 5	9A 0	9A10	9A10	10A10	10A50	11 0	11 10	2A10	12 5	12 5
Dolgelley arr	9 26	...	3 59	3 59	...	...	4 56	5 20	8 53	9 26	...
Towyn	..	..							10 0		
Aberdovey									10 7		
Barmouth	10 5	3 28	4 30	4 30	4 52	5 31	5 25	5 45	9 23	10 5	10K 1
Harlech	10 54	3 52	5 18	..	5 34	5 56	5 51	6 25	...	10 54	
Portmadoc	11 21	4 10	5 40	..	5 58	6 19	6 16	6 42	...	11 21	
Criccieth	11 35	4 23	5 49	..	6 9	6 29	6 26	6 52	...	11 35	
Pwllheli	11 58	4 48	6 10	..	6 30	6 45	6 46	7 12	...	11 58	

WEEK DAYS / SUNDAYS

	R	S	R	RD E	S	R	R	M
	am	am	am	am	am	am	pm	pm
Pwllheli dep	5 35	7A20	8 45	9A35	9A35	11 30	12 45	4y 0
Criccieth	5 52	7A50	9 5	10A 3	10A 3	11 50	1 5	4y22
Portmadoc	6 2	8A 2	9 15	10A16	10A16	12 2	1 17	4y35
Harlech	6 23	8A23	9 35	10A35	10A35	12 28	1 44	5y 0
Barmouth	7 18	8A50	10 20	11A 0	11A 0	1 10	2 35	5y32
Dolgelley	7 45	..	10 48	..	..	1 37	3 4	4y58
PADDINGTON arr	2F12	3 25	5 15	6 0	6 20	8 35	10 25	5V10

A or A Seats can be reserved in advance on payment of a fee of 1s. 0d. per seat (see page 26)
B 1st and 3rd Class Sleeping Car (limited accommodation) Carmarthen to Paddington
C 1st and 3rd Class Sleeping Car (limited accommodation) Paddington to Ruabon
D Cambrian Coast Express
E Except Saturdays
F On Saturdays arrive 2 22 pm
G Saturdays only and runs 25th June to 10th September inclusive
J Via Gobowen and Oswestry
K Via Gobowen, Oswestry and Machynlleth

M 1st and 3rd Class Sleeping Car (limited accommodation) Ruabon to Paddington
N Via Carmarthen
P Except Saturday nights/Sunday mornings. For Sunday mornings see first column Sundays
Q Except Saturday nights
R Refreshment Car provided, in some cases for a portion of the journey only
S Saturdays only
T Saturdays only and will not run after 10th September
V am. On Saturday mornings 23rd July to 13th August inclusive, arrive 4 5 am by changing at Wolverhampton

Y On Saturdays arrive 8 25 pm
Z 1st and 3rd Class Sleeping Car (limited accommodation), Paddington to Carmarthen
a On Saturdays arrive 8 8 pm
b On Saturdays arr 3 25 pm
c Commences 25th June
d On Saturdays depart 5 45 pm
y Via Machynlleth and Welshpool. Or Saturdays depart Dolgelley 5 20 pm
* am
‡ pm

PASSENGERS SHOULD ASCERTAIN IF CHANGE OF TRAIN IS NECESSARY

116.   The bay on the right was intended for trains on the Llanidloes-Brecon line, but most had terminated at Moat Lane Junction for many years. The mill building in the background is a reminder that the town had once been a noted textile centre. (Lens of Sutton coll.)

117.   An eastward panorama on 14th July 1966 includes the end of the loop and the bridge carrying the road to Kerry. The industrial building is one of many still standing in the town as a reminder of its past. There is also an impressive selection of contemporary chapels. (C.L.Caddy)

CAMBRIAN COAST EXPRESS
RESTAURANT CAR SERVICE (¶)

LONDON, ABERDOVEY, TOWYN, BARMOUTH, PWLLHELI and ABERYSTWYTH

WEEK DAYS

		E am	S am
London (Paddington) ..	..dep	11A10	11A10
		pm	pm
Banbury	{ arr	12 30	12 37
	{ dep	12 33	12 40
Leamington Spa General	{ arr	12 55	1 6
	{ dep	12 58	1 9
Birmingham	{ arr	1 31	1 43
(Snow Hill)	{ dep	1 35	1 48
Wolverhampton	{ arr	1 58	2 8
(Low Level)	{ dep	2 5	2 15
Wellington	{ arr	2 29	..
	{ dep	2 30	..
Shrewsbury	{ arr	2 47	..
	{ dep	2 54	..
Welshpool	..arr	3 30	3 30
Newtown	.. ,,	4 5	4 5
Moat Lane Junction ..	.. ,,	4 14	4 14
Machynlleth	.. ,,	4 58	4 58

		E am	S am
Machynlleth	..dep	5 10	5 10
Penhelig Halt	..arr	5 32	5 32
Aberdovey	.. ,,	5 36	5 36
Towyn	.. ,,	5 43	5 43
Tonfanau.	.. ,,	5 47	5 47
Llwyngwril	.. ,,	5 59	5 59
Fairbourne	.. ,,	6 7	6 7
Morfa Mawddach.. ..	.. ,,	6 11	6 11
Barmouth	.. ,,	6 18	6 18
Dyffryn-Ardudwy ..	.. ,,	6 30	6 30
Harlech..	.. ,,	6 45	6 45
Penrhyndeudraeth ..	.. ,,	6 57	6 57
Portmadoc	.. ,,	7 8	7 8
Criccieth	.. ,,	7 20	7 20
Afon Wen	.. ,,	7 26	7 26
Penychain B	.. ,,	7 31	7 31
Pwllheli..	.. ,,	7 40	7 40

		E am	S am
Machynlleth	..dep	5 0	5 0
Dovey Junction	..arr	5 7	5 7
Borth	.. ,,	5 22	5 22
Aberystwyth	.. ,,	5 45	5 45

		E am	S am
Aberystwyth	..dep	9A45	9A45
Borth..	.. ,,	10 A 5	10A 5
Dovey Junction.	..arr	10 22	10 22

		E am	S am
Pwllheli..	..dep	7A35	..
Penychain B	.. ,,	7 43	..
Afon Wen	.. ,,	7 53	..
Criccieth	.. ,,	8 A 0	..
Portmadoc	.. ,,	8A13	..
Penrhyndeudraeth ..	.. ,,	8A23	..
Harlech..	.. ,,	8A42	..
Llanbedr and Pensarn	.. ,,	8 50	..
Dyffryn-Ardudwy ..	.. ,,	9 0	..
Barmouth	.. ,,	9A20	..
Morfa Mawddach ..	.. ,,	9A27	9A20
Fairbourne	.. ,,	9A30	9A23
Llwyngwril	.. ,,	9A39	9A32
Tonfanau	.. ,,	9 47	9 41
Towyn	.. ,,	9A53	9A48
Aberdovey	.. ,,	10 A 0	9A56
Penhelig Halt	.. ,,	10 3	10 1
Dovey Junction	..arr	10 17	10 17

		E am	S am
Dovey Junction	..dep	10A28	10A30
Machynlleth	.. ,,	10A37	10A39
Moat Lane Junction ..	.. ,,	11 22	11 25
Newtown	.. ,,	11 31	11 34
		pm	pm
Welshpool	.. ,,	12 3	12 10
Shrewsbury	{ arr	12 41	..
	{ dep	12 49	..
Wolverhampton	{ arr	1 27	1 29
(Low Level)	{ dep	1 35	1 35
Birmingham	{ arr	1 56	1 56
(Snow Hill)	{ dep	2 0	2 0
Leamington Spa	{ arr	2 24	2 28
General	{ dep	2 25	2 30
Banbury	{ arr	2 52	3 1
	{ dep	2 55	3 4
London (Paddington) ..	..arr	4 15	4 26

A—Seats can be reserved in advance on payment of a fee of 2s. 0d. per seat (see page 27).
B—For Pwllheli Holiday Camp.
E—Except Saturdays.
S—Saturdays only.
¶—Restaurant Car available between London (Paddington) and Wolverhampton, in each direction.

June 1962

THROUGH TRAIN SERVICE

MANCHESTER and ABERYSTWYTH and BARMOUTH

(Via Whitchurch)

SATURDAYS ONLY
Runs until 1st September inclusive

		am	
Manchester (Piccadilly).. .. ..dep	..	11A 5	..
Stockport (Edgeley) .... ,,	......	11 17	......
Crewe .. .. ,,	..	12 3	..
Whitchurch .... ,,	......	12 35	......
Ellesmere .. .. ,,	..	12 58	..
Oswestry .... ,,	......	1 30	......
Welshpool .. .. ,,	..	2 0	..
Newtown ....arr	......	2 28	......
Machynlleth .. .. ,,	..	3 18	..
Aberdovey..........................arr	......	3 59	......
Towyn.. .. .. ,,	..	4 8	..
Fairbourne..................... ,,	......	4 30	......
Barmouth .. .. ,,	..	4 40	..
Borth ....arr	......	3 49	......
Aberystwyth .. .. ,,	..	4 10	..

SATURDAYS ONLY
Commences 30th June

		am	
Aberystwyth .. ..dep	..	10A55	..
Borth .... ,,	......	11A15	......
Barmouth .. ..dep	..	10A35	..
Fairbourne .... ,,	......	10A43	......
Towyn.. .. .. ,,	..	11A 8	..
Aberdovey .... ,,	......	11A16	......
Machynlleth .. ..dep	..	11A54	..
Newtown .... ,,	......	1 3	......
Welshpool .. ..arr	..	1 28	..
Oswestry .... ,,	......	2 7	......
Ellesmere .. .. ,,	..	2 35	..
Whitchurch .... ,,	......	3 5	......
Crewe .. .. ,,	......	3 39	......
Stockport (Edgeley)..................... ,,	......	4 19	......
Manchester (Piccadilly) .. .. ,,	..	4 32	..

A—Seats can be reserved in advance on payment of a fee of 2s. 0d. per seat

June 1962

118.   The box is seen on the same day. Its frame was shortened from 54 to 35 levers subsequently and it closed on 21st October 1988, when a radio system at Machynlleth took over. This operated as far east as Hookagate. (C.L.Caddy)

Other views of this station and a large scale map can be found in our *Brecon to Newtown* album.

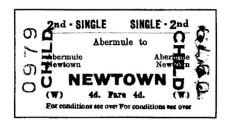

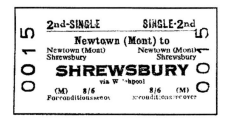

119.   The 15.00 from Aberystwyth to Shrewsbury was worked by no. 150124 on 7th September 1989. British Rail Engineering Ltd. produced these units in 2-car and 3-car formations in 1985-86. (T.Heavyside)

120.   After a very long interval, a steam locomotive crept across Barmouth Bridge on 15th June 1991. No. 75069 is returning and is surrounded by historic buildings. The cast iron brackets under the roof on the left include the initials CR and the station retains its originality. To enable the service to be improved to hourly, the entire route from Shrewsbury to Aberystwyth was closed from 19th to 27th April 2008 for radio signalling alterations. (H.Ballantyne)

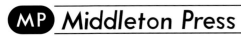
MP Middleton Press

EVOLVING THE ULTIMATE RAIL ENCYCLOPEDIA

Easebourne Lane, Midhurst, West Sussex.
GU29 9AZ   Tel:01730 813169

www.middletonpress.co.uk   email:info@middletonpress.co.uk
A-978 0 906520 B- 978 1 873793 C- 978 1 901706 D-978 1 904474 E - 978 1 906008

OOP Out of print at time of printing - Please check availability   BROCHURE AVAILABLE SHOWING NEW TITLES